THE LITTLE BLACK BOOK OF

KAMA SUTRA

The Classic Guide to Lovemaking

L. L. LONG

ILLUSTRATED BY BIL DONOVAN

PETER PAUPER PRESS, INC.
WHITE PLAINS, NEW YORK

For my Lazarus

Special thanks to Inner Traditions International,
for permission to use excerpts from The Complete Kama Sutra,
translated by Alain Daniélou.

Designed by Heather Zschock

Illustrations copyright © 2006 Bil Donovan/www.artscounselinc.com

Visit us at www.peterpauper.com

THE LITTLE
BLACK BOOK OF
KAMA SUTRA

*If the couple's conduct is in accordance with
the teachings of the* Kama Sutra, *their life
will be a success from an erotic point of view.
The partners will always be satisfied with
each other and their spirit will not be
touched by any desire to be unfaithful.*

DEVADATTA SHASTRI,
Hindi commentator, as quoted in the *Kama Sutra*

AUTHOR'S NOTE:

These texts are thousands of years old. Many were
transmitted orally before being transcribed into their
original languages of Sanskrit and Arabic. It's likely that
bits have been lost to history, or that the meaning of
certain passages has changed, either accidentally or by
design. Numerous translations add a further layer of
uncertainty about the original meaning of the text. In
the spirit of the imperfect art of oral tradition, I've
taken the license of infusing the *Kama Sutra* with a
modern sensibility, and inferring actions and concepts
that aren't spelled out in the text.

—L. L. L.

CONTENTS

INTRODUCTION

Why We Should Care about a 1,600-Year-Old Book

Why indeed? One can find sex manuals in every good bookstore, and explicit articles describing sexual techniques and acrobatic positions in every fashion magazine. There is, clearly, nothing new under the sun in the sex department.

Why should we return to the ancient text of the *Kama Sutra of Vatsyayana*, with its *lingams* and *yonis,* its unfamiliar words and customs? Because, readers, the *Kama Sutra* is the source from which all subsequent sex manuals spring. It's the original, the real deal. Accept no imitations. Go to the source. And because, despite its quaint language, the *Kama Sutra* is a work of great poetry. Sure, you can engage in Position #16 that you read about in your favorite magazine, and you can tangle yourselves up as though you were playing an erotic version of *Twister*, but how much more delightful will your experience be if you retitle your encounter *The Position of the Queen of Heaven*? Poetry matters, folks, even in sex. Especially in sex.

This book puts it all in modern context for today's lovers—so you and your partner can have just as much fun as the freewheeling ancients.

WHILE YOU STILL HAVE YOUR CLOTHES ON

A little historical context. The original text of the *Kama Sutra* is actually an edited anthology, with commentary, of several earlier works compiled in the fourth century C.E. by a high-caste and learned man named Vatsyayana. Concerned that the ancient erotic texts had become difficult to access, he sought to combine these into a single volume. One imagines the arduous nature of the research, especially sixteen centuries before the invention of the Internet, although Vatsyayana assures the reader that he has verified all practices described in the text through personal experience.

The original text is a comprehensive manual on how to be a good citizen in fourth-century India—a surprisingly liberated society. It is addressed to the equivalent of a metrosexual male. He's expected to be cultured, prosperous, dress well, act the part of raconteur at parties, and be good at sports. Our expectations haven't changed much, have they?

A man must realize himself on three interdependent levels, which are virtue [dharma], wealth [artha], and love [kāma], harmonizing them in such a way that none is prejudicial to the others.

YASHODHARA, twelfth-century commentary on the *Kama Sutra* (This commentary is included in modern translations.)

We know why you bought this book, so we'll skip over the virtue and prosperity and go straight to the "love." Suffice it to say that the *Kama Sutra* strongly advocates a balanced life, and suggests that a fulfilling love life is only possible when other aspects of one's life are in harmony. That's good advice, even today.

Many of the practices described in the original text might strike us as odd: There are extensive sections on the secret language signified by bites and scratches. At some level, we can dismiss these as cultural peculiarities of another age—but they contained a deeper meaning in their context. Visible marks were badges of possession and erotic prowess and were sported proudly by lovers of both genders. Likewise, a modern reader may find the fact that the text is addressed to a male a jarring anachronism, but Vatsyayana consistently counsels the reader on how best to please his lady, and he encouraged women to familiarize themselves with the text. At the root of it is the desire for pleasure and for a lucky few—spiritual union.

The highest pleasure is the reciprocal discovery by man and woman of the natural differences of the lower part of their bodies. . . .

YASHODHARA

To begin with, Vatsyayana advises that everyone (this means you!) should be studying *The Sixty-Four Arts*, a laundry list of skills that both men and women were expected to master, including (but by no means limited to) conjuring, puns and poetry, chess, and—naturally—erotic arts. For the purposes of this book, however, we'll assume that our readers are already experts in these varied arts or their contemporary equivalents.

 Finally, we'll also be delving into other ancient erotic works of Asia: *Ananga-Ranga*, *The Perfumed Garden*, and portions of the Chinese *T'ung Hsüan Tzu*, or *Tao*. Nineteenth-century scholar Sir Richard Burton thoughtfully anthologized the *Kama*

Sutra, *Ananga-Ranga*, and *The Perfumed Garden* for his repressed Victorian readership—they're three scandals in one! However, it's important to note that they are, in fact, three distinctly differ-

ent volumes, reflecting the cultural values of their ages—and each has merit on its own. We urge you to seek out these texts for further study.

Also of India, *Ananga-Ranga* is a work of the fifteenth or sixteenth century. This world was very different from the open-minded culture of the original *Kama Sutra*—a world of gender segregation and arranged marriages. The author seeks to offer sexual variety to married couples to prevent boredom and ensure fidelity.

The Perfumed Garden belongs to the Islamic world of the late 1400s. Although its author, Sheikh Nefzawi, is something of a chauvinist, it's a work of both humor and poetry, and makes a valuable contribution to the world of erotic literature.

Our final stop on our erotic world tour is the Chinese text *T'ung Hsüan Tzu*. The Chinese philosophy of Tao again emphasizes the need for balance in all aspects of life. Sex is a way to bring the disparate elements of yin and yang into perfect balance.

While these four texts belong to another age, lovemaking is ageless. Let us allow the works of the ancient masters to both arouse and uplift us.

It has been said that, "The man accomplished in riches, love, and virtue effortlessly attains the maximum of bliss in this world and the next."

VATSYAYANA

setting the scene

Sexuality is essential for the survival of man, just as food is necessary for bodily health, and on them depend both virtue and wealth.

VATSYAYANA

THE BODY TEMPLE

Good sex doesn't just happen. The most skilled lovers of the ancient and modern world know that lovemaking begins hours—even days—before coitus occurs. Great lovers instinctively engage the most sensitive sex organ—the brain—before any body parts come into contact. Customs may change (we no longer chew betel nut after meals to sweeten our breath), but the basic rules of engagement haven't changed much in the last two millennia. Vatsyayana's text is explicit in its description of the rules of diet, hygiene, and conduct governing polite society.

Translate Vatsyayana's quaint-sounding advice regarding the frequent changing of underwear and shaving off of pubic hair (both advocated), and we are left with this truth: the occasional sweaty encounter after a day hiking or at the beach notwithstanding, good personal hygiene is important for good sex. It demonstrates respect for yourself and for your partner. Would you want to make love to someone who doesn't respect his or

her body enough to keep it clean? Neither would our fourth-century metrosexual.

For a man to be successful with women,
he must pay them marked attention.
His dress should be neat, his figure graceful, and
his looks should mark him out from
his fellows. He must be truthful and sincere,
generous, and brave. He should not
be vain, and he should make himself
agreeable in company.

SHEIKH NEFZAWI

Even in the days before hot tubs and indoor plumbing, Vatsyayana is also aware that mutual grooming can be powerfully arousing. To set the scene:

- **Be sure the bathroom is clean and warm.** In summer, ensure adequate ventilation with a fan or open a window.

- **Have lots of fluffy towels handy.** Use a hot-water bottle to warm them up.

- Sweet-smelling—and hypoallergenic—products will ensure lots of bubbly fun.

- Candles set a romantic mood, but always take care when burning candles to keep them away from curtains and towels.

- Girls, work up a lather by carefully shaving your man's face. Slow and steady wins the day here.

- Guys can try shaving their ladies' legs with long, sexy strokes starting at the ankle.

He should . . . loosen her girdle and the knot of her dress, and turning up her lower garment should shampoo the joints of her naked thighs . . . but he should not at this time begin actual congress.

VATSYAYANA

BEYOND HEAD & SHOULDERS

The Art of the Shampoo

One of the most charming—and frustrating—
aspects of the *Kama Sutra* is the elastic and elusive
meanings of many of the words used in it. For
example, depending on the context, the term
"shampoo" can indicate actual washing with soap,
or it can mean a non-erotic massage. Or, it can
have more sexual overtones. Prostitutes or people

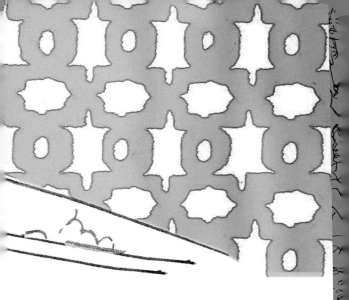

of questionable moral character were often referred to as "shampooers." The vagueness of the terminology lends a certain license to the practices it describes. We are at liberty to interpret the instructions as we wish, according to circumstances. So, in some cases, a shampoo in the modern sense might be called for, but no one would blame you if you reverted to the archaic meaning and decided to offer your partner a sensual massage!

SENSES AND SENSIBILITY

The citizen enters the chamber of love . . .
which is carefully decorated, ornamented with
flowers, and perfumed with scented smoke.
He invites the woman to drink with him. . . .
Then comes vocal and instrumental music. . . .

VATSYAYANA

The ancients had the five senses covered. You should, too. Sights, sounds, scents, tastes, and textures can all enhance the sexual experience.

- **Lighting should be soft.** Candlelight imparts a warm glow to skin and surroundings. Everyone usually looks and feels better in candlelight. It's more inviting to tumble into a well-appointed boudoir. Stow away the piles of laundry and magazines. And turn off that TV!

- **When trying to set a romantic mood,** it's usually best to stay away from harsh or loud music. Unless you and your beloved share a mutual fantasy involving marching bands, it's probably the wrong time to showcase your collection of John Philip Sousa CDs. And what about suggestive conversation?

He amuses her with funny stories, making her laugh, and speaks hintingly of indecent and secret things.

VATSYAYANA

- **Scent is very personal.** Experiment with what pleases you and your partner. The ancients favored sandalwood incense, but the aromas of ylang-ylang, patchouli, and rose are also believed to possess aphrodisiac properties. Scents can be evocative all on their own. Does a whiff of your lover's cologne send a tingle through you? Or does the smell of oranges take you back to a romantic escapade in Provence?

When a woman inhales the scent
with which a man is perfumed she
loses her power of control. . . .

SHEIKH NEFZAWI

- **A shared meal is often a sensual prelude to love.** The act of feeding each other can be powerfully erotic . . . take turns with sexy strawberries or other bite-size tidbits. Or have some fun with chocolate and whipped cream (best practiced in the kitchen or bathroom). Note, however, that rich foods and alcohol inhibit desire—you might find that you or your beloved doze off before the fun starts.

- **Aside from the occasional alfresco tryst or romp on the kitchen floor,** most of your lovemaking will likely occur in a bed. Your bed is your friend. Comfortable furnishings are a must, and your attention to texture will be appreciated. Ditch the scratchy, pilly sheets and invest in some high thread count linens. Like layered clothing, layered bedding works well. You throw off the layers you don't need, or snuggle down on chilly nights. Throw in a touch of satin (not too much or you *will* wind up on the floor!), some interesting texture on the covers (matelasse or chenille throws), and you're good to go. Pillows should be the best quality you can afford. This will pay off in a good night's sleep *after* you've exhausted all the positions in this book and invented a few of your own.

A word about temperature: The best guide is your own comfort level. This is another case where moderation should be your watchword. Keep the room pleasantly warm in winter, pleasantly cool in summer.

THERE ARE NO ERRONEOUS ZONES

It's All Good

Think of your entire body as one giant erogenous zone controlled by the largest and most important erogenous zone—your brain. Every inch of your skin (the body's largest and arguably the most sensitive organ) can be teased and pleased in some way. You're limited only by your own imagination, and your partner's.

Through the power of imagination, the anticipation of romance can be almost as sweet as the act itself. In the right setting, the subtlest caress or glance is powerfully intoxicating. Even a casual or "accidental" brush against your lover at a party can be considered a form of embrace (see page 37).

- **Hair:** Touch your own in a sensuous way. Ruffle your lover's. The scalp has many nerve endings. Try a feathery light touch.

- **Face:** Here's another area rich in nerve endings. A finger pressed to the lips, or gently tracing their shape, can quickly arouse your partner—in any setting.

- **Neck and shoulders:** Trace the curve of her neck with your fingertip. Lightly knead his shoulders while he's reading the paper.

- **Arms and hands:** The inside of the wrist and the soft inside of the arm are especially sensitive. Try reading your lover's palm. What do you see there?

Overcome with passion, she caresses
him with one hand; with the other arm,
she arouses him by touching him and
massaging him, as though by chance.

VATSYAYANA

- **Torso:** Enjoy the curve of her hips. Belly-button play can be both fun and sexy. Don't leave out the back or the playful curves and rich nerve endings of the buttocks. Both are wonderful terrain for massage—with or without clothes!

- **Legs and feet:** Many find the backs of the knees especially receptive to touch. And feet . . . well, feet just drive some people wild. Just be careful of "over-tickling" your partner. While sex is fun, and can be funny, respect your partner's boundaries when he or she says, "enough!"

God has granted us the kiss on the mouth, the cheeks and the neck, as also the sucking of luscious lips. . . . He has embellished with breasts a woman's chest . . . and her cheeks with jewels and brilliants. He has also given her eyes which inspire love. . . .

SHEIKH NEFZAWI

HERE'S THE RUB
Where a Little Massage Can Lead

It's no secret that most of us enjoy a relaxing back rub, or that a massage can be a languid prelude to lovemaking—or provide non-erotic intimacy if one partner is too tired for sex. Don't limit your therapeutic touch just to the back, however! Possibilities abound for the relief of tired feet, stressed-out scalps, or exercise-knotted muscles.

Massage is different from tickling, although the end result might be the same. And when in doubt, always go with a lighter touch.

A FEW BASIC MASSAGE STROKES

- **Compression** is the application of firm pressure from the heel of the hand or loosely clenched fists. On the arm or leg, compression can also be a full-handed squeezing motion. On the fingers and toes, compression is applied with small squeezes between the forefingers and thumbs.

- **Effleurage** is the signature stroke of Swedish massage. It's the application of long, sweeping strokes for relaxation—perfect for the arms, legs, and back. Allow the weight of your body to provide the force to your hands, rather than drawing solely on the strength of your arms and fingers.

- **Petrissage** involves grasping, lifting, and kneading the muscle with the whole hand. Avoid focusing too much pressure between the ends of the fingers and thumbs—no pinching! Use on long muscles with a "belly," like calves, thighs, and biceps.

- **Circular friction** is applied with the thumbs, fingers, palms, heels of hands, or loose fists. Use small circular movements to allow the skin to glide over the underlying muscle or to move a superficial muscle over a deeper muscle or bone.

Use fragrant oils and lotions to enhance the massage (check for allergies first). Lubricants soften the skin and allow your hands to glide over your partner's body, warming as you go. Do consider the properties of any fragrance you choose to use. Lavender is well-known for its relaxing and healing properties. Citrus scents are typically lively and energizing—ideal for a morning massage that will keep you going for the whole day.

BIRDS DO IT, BEES DO IT

Some would argue that seduction and flirtation are lost arts. Surely not! Courtship dances are as old—older, even—as recorded history. Is seduction hard-wired into our psyches?

> *... God has created woman with her beauty and appetizing flesh: ... He has endowed her with hair, waist, and throat, breasts which swell, and amorous gestures which increase desire.*

SHEIKH NEFZAWI

The ancient texts are full of advice on seduction. While teaching mynah birds to speak may not be your idea of a hot date, the *Kama Sutra* describes party games, gambling, and outdoor pursuits that wouldn't seem so out of place today. Much foreplay occurs in social settings amidst teasing on both sides. Secret meetings also abound—a sexy custom we should consider reviving.

Love letters carried by intermediaries flew back and forth. How about a handwritten note instead of a hastily jotted e-mail? Or a poem to your beloved? Not a poet? Consult the experts: Donne, Shakespeare, or the Bible.

The *Kama Sutra* is your best source on playing "hard to get," as the cultural norm of the age was for women to publicly approach seduction with diffidence. This led to frequent exchanges of gifts—to the benefit of the women!

You can indicate your intentions with the smallest of gestures in the most public of places: a thrown kiss, a glance, a whispered promise.

When they are alone she shows her feelings,
but does not let other people know them.
She dissimulates in public, guarding
her secret from others.

VATSYAYANA

embraceable you

*When the potter starts his wheel moving,
the speed, initially slow, increases little by little,
then slows down and stops. It appears that
it is the same in exciting a woman from
the beginning to the end.*

VATSYAYANA

Not surprisingly, the ancients begin their discussion of foreplay with the various forms of embrace. They also note that many embraces take place outside a strictly sexual context—although others are very intimate and obviously occur as part of the sex act itself.

We'll present these embraces described in the *Kama Sutra* roughly in order from the least intimate—an embrace that you might enjoy during a walk in the park—to the most intimate (the kind that typically occurs only behind closed doors).

The Touching, or Contact Embrace

When a man under some pretext or other goes in front of or alongside a woman and touches her body with his own, it is called the "touching embrace."

You "accidentally" brush past an enticing stranger at a party. You linger a little too close to your lover in the theater lobby. In full view of the world, you're enjoying the most basic of embraces.

The Bruising, or Piercing Embrace

The Bruising, or Piercing Embrace

When a woman . . . bends down, as if to pick up something, and pierces, as it were, a man sitting or standing, with her breasts, and the man in return takes hold of them, it is called a "piercing embrace."

Sometimes it's deliberate on the woman's part: She positions herself in such a manner that indicates that she'd like her lover to fondle her breasts. Or sometimes the guy just takes the initiative.

The Baring/Rubbing Embrace

In the darkness, if people are present, or otherwise in an isolated place, they stroll slowly, showing their bodies to each other, not just for an instant, but for some time.

This embrace can also be called the "sneak peek." Go ahead—try a little flash in a public place—if you dare.

The Squeezing/Pressing Embrace

Leaning against a wall or pillar, he presses his erect organ against her.

There's no mistaking what's on your partner's mind when he gives you this unambiguous signal!

Climbing a Tree

Hungry for a cuddle at the end of the day? This sweetly sexy embrace allows for lots of body contact. Don't be surprised if your partner steals a little booty squeeze while you're trying to "climb" him.

She embraces him with her arm across his back. Her other arm clings to his shoulder and neck. With a slight sigh, she makes an effort to climb onto him and to kiss him, just as if she were climbing a tree.

*The Squeezing/
Pressing Embrace*

The Embrace of Brows or Forehead

Face to face, gazing into each other's eyes, their brows join, the one against the other.

It's time for your close-up. This embrace is surprisingly intimate, and can take place anywhere. Your desire will be revealed in your eyes.

The Embrace of the Breasts

When a man places his breast between the breasts of a woman and presses her with it, it is called the "embrace of the breasts."

A straightforward upper-body embrace—and an excuse to touch your lover's nipples. But who will mind if the lower halves of your bodies get in on the act, too?

The Embrace of the Thighs

This one's a classic "make out" position, beloved of high-school students of all ages. For a truly nostalgic experience, try it on the couch with your clothes on, but skip the part where your parents catch you in the act.

When one of two lovers presses forcibly one or both of the thighs of the other between his or her own, it is called "the embrace of the thighs."

The Liana

Encircling her lover like a liana . . . she bends her face toward him for a kiss and then withdraws with a small sigh. Assured and showing off her beauty, she seems to entwine around him like a liana.

Theatrical and teasing, this embrace sends a mixed message. A few kisses and caresses should clear up the confusion.

The Mixing of Rice and Sesame

Both lying with arms and legs entwined, they rub against each other and become deeply entangled.

You languorously wind around each other . . . perhaps your passion is spent or maybe you're just getting started.

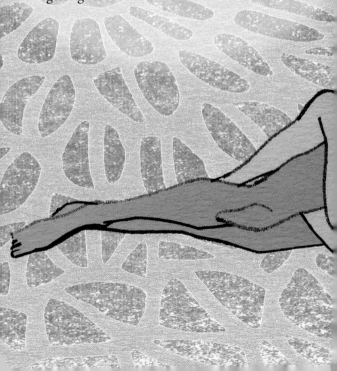

The Mixing of Milk and Water

Whereas in the **Rice and Sesame** embrace, you are still two distinct entities, when milk and water mix, it becomes impossible to tell them apart. In your passion, you have lost the sense of where your body ends and where your lover's begins. Even if you are not yet united by the act of intercourse, you move as one.

Blinded by desire, unable to wait, they press against each other with the same passion, face to face, whether seated or lying down.

The Embrace of the Jaghana

When the man presses the jaghana or middle part of the woman's body against his own, and mounts upon her to practise [sic] . . . the hair of the woman being loose and flowing, it is called the "embrace of the jaghana."

Jaghana is one of those maddeningly ambiguous words that Vatsyayana loved to use. He could be describing any part of the body between the belly button and the knees, but who are we kidding? Maybe the only thing keeping you from the act itself in this unrestrained simulation is your undies.

oral arguments
kissing and other pleasures

*When a boy and girl experience such a shock at
their first kiss, they become mad with desire. . . .
In their kisses, they find love's oneness, a feeling so
strong that they can no longer see each other's faults.
Young people kissing become radiant. The kiss is
the gateway to bliss and amorous experience.*

DEVADATTA SHASTRI

Although not every kiss is erotic, kissing is a natural component of eroticism. We kiss before, during, and after sex. Most often, we kiss our partners' mouths, but the most sensual part of the body to kiss is . . . wherever it feels good. Revel in the taste of your lover.

Is there ever an inappropriate time or place to kiss? We can't think of one. From the "good morning" peck to the most passionate rip-your-clothes-off necking, there are kisses for every mood and every occasion. Apparently, the ancients agree.

As with embraces, the kisses are arranged in order of ascending eroticism, culminating in utter abandon of the lovers to their ardor. We can imagine a courtship of kisses designed to arouse even the most diffident of lovers. Also described are a series of situational kisses, including the kiss you would give to an image of your lover. If you are in the habit of kissing your lover's photo, know that it's called **The Kiss Showing Intention.**

The *Kama Sutra* also discusses oral sex—fellatio and cunnilingus—about which Vatsyayana is coyly inconclusive, stating alternately that it is "not recommended"; then, throwing up his hands, declaring that if it feels good, do it. We can only conclude that as a detailed chapter is devoted to oral pleasure and its techniques, it must have been commonly practiced, and most likely accepted.

Let's get smoochin'!

*Once the sexual impulse is
fully awakened, a day waiting for
one's lover seems an eternity.*

DEVADATTA SHASTRI

TURNING UP THE HEAT

*Desire, affection, love create a lasting state
of mind, through which the boy and girl,
stimulated by caresses and kisses, abandon themselves wholeheartedly to the act of love.*

RUPAGOSVAMI

The Nominal Kiss

This is a light kiss, straight lip-to-lip, with no
tongue involvement.

The Vibrant, or Throbbing Kiss

Feeling bolder, one of you parts your lips slightly
to allow your lover the barest taste of the inside of
your lip.

The Rubbing, or Touching Kiss

As you ease into the kiss, you also begin to explore
your lover's lips with your tongue, closing your
eyes and clasping hands.

The Straight, or Equal Kiss

This is a no-frills, face-to-face kiss.

The Crosswise, or Bent Kiss

As naturally as falling in love, the lovers turn their heads slightly to the side to kiss, in a Hollywood-style kiss. This kiss is often employed during intercourse and embraces, as the pose is so natural.

The Turned, or Reverse Kiss

Your lover tilts your chin and kisses you tenderly, but with ardor. Often used after a theatrical declaration of love.

The Pressed Kiss

This kiss can occur in two stages: as you trace the contours of your partner's mouth, possibly having your finger(s) licked and sucked by your partner, you swoop in for a deep, long kiss. This is especially sensual because your lips, face, and fingertips are loaded with ultra-sensitive nerve endings.

The Turned, or Reverse Kiss

ROAM IF YOU WANT TO

The *Kama Sutra* doesn't leave off kissing at just the mouth. It advocates kissing anywhere on the body. Kisses that land elsewhere (i.e., not on the mouth) are called "special kisses," and the following techniques are employed:

> *Sama* [equal] *is done on the brow or elsewhere, on the thigh joint, the armpits, the pubis, neither too hard nor too soft.*

> *Pidita* [pressed], *on the cheeks, the armpits, the sexual region.*

> *Ashchita* [devouring], *on the brow, the chin, and the body up to the armpits.*

> *Mridu* [delicate], *lightly touching the eyes.*

> YASHODHARA

And why stop there? Don't forget the neck, back, shoulders, buttocks, knees, and elbows—or anywhere else you can think of where your partner might like to be kissed.

The *Kama Sutra* also describes charming kissing games and competitions designed to inflame the lovers into a frenzy of passion.

> *The aim of these games is to fire passion,*
> *establishing physical intimacy between*
> *the boy and girl which will lead to coition.*
> *It is not so in every case, however. If the*
> *boy and girl are very ardent, they have no*
> *time to lose before getting to copulation.*

DEVADATTA SHASTRI

In other words, if you're rarin' to go, quit playing games and get down to business!

The Fifth Hold

This kiss really grabs your lover's attention. Using a two-handed approach, one or both partners cups the other's face before leaning in for a kiss.

VIVE LA FRANCE

"French kissing" isn't French (and you didn't invent it, even if you wish you had). The *Kama Sutra* outlines many techniques of lip and tongue play, including a mock "combat" of tongues. French kissing can be deeply arousing, and its variations are many, from the most delicate tongue tracery along your lover's lips to a full-tongue exploration that mimics the rhythm and intensity of intercourse.

SOME FRENCH KISSING POINTERS:

- Flavors of tobacco, alcohol, and spicy foods are a turn-off. If you think necking is in your future, err on the side of a quick brushing of your teeth, or a mint.

- Most people like to start out *slowly*. Unless you know your partner likes to be kissed this way, don't begin by sticking your whole tongue into her mouth.

- Although bumping teeth might be cause for a laugh, it can hurt! Also, be gentle with lip and tongue nibbles. The abundance of nerve endings will supply all the sensation your partner needs. The *Kama Sutra* names these little nibbling kisses the vagabond.

- Come up for air once an hour.

TIMING IS EVERYTHING— SITUATIONAL KISSES

Up to now, we've been concerned with *techniques* of kissing. Once you've mastered the kisses of the *Kama Sutra* and invented a few new ones, you can think about when to use each one.

Kiss that Kindles Love

Ladies, are you feeling frisky, but lover boy is too pooped to pop? A few kisses and some strategic caresses should bring him deliciously awake and ready to play.

The Kiss that Awakens

Turnabout is fair play! If you've hit the hay early, but your lover has other plans, he might nuzzle you gently awake to let you know exactly what he has in mind. Feigning sleep in order to elicit this behavior isn't out of the question either, and it sure beats waking up to an alarm clock.

The Kiss of Encouragement/Kiss that Turns Away

Kiss of Encouragement/
Kiss that Turns Away

Although they didn't have football in Vatsyayana's day, there were plenty of other distractions to pre-occupy the men of ancient India. This is just the kiss to get his attention refocused on what *really* matters. Tough day in Rajasthan, darling? This kiss also works on a man who's in a bad mood—it's difficult to stay grumpy when your lover is caressing your nipples or genitals.

Demonstrative Kiss

When at night at a theatre . . . a man coming up to a woman kisses a finger of her hand . . . it is called a "demonstrative kiss."

This is another kiss of intention. It might look decorous and demure, but it's loaded! He might be kissing your hand, but he's telling you with his eyes and his lips what he'd rather be kissing. This kiss says, "Wait 'til I get you alone."

SEXUAL PARITY

Although the *Kama Sutra* was written from the perspective of educating a young nobleman, it certainly wasn't a man's world! Then as now, women were active participants in sex, not mere objects of desire.

The differences in male and female sexual responses are acknowledged: women typically are slower to become aroused, but, once aroused, remain so longer.

The man is also expected to make every effort to please his partner, including delaying his orgasm to coincide with the woman's, and to continue to pleasure her as long as she desires it.

Whatever the circumstances, open or secret kisses cause both man and woman wonderful pleasure. When lovers kiss, their purpose is to draw close to each other, to develop love and mutual trust.

DEVADATTA SHASTRI

ACQUIRED TASTES
Oral Sex, *Kama Sutra* Style

> *When two actors do a job together,*
> *the job accomplished is one. Each pursues*
> *his own goal, which is, however, connected*
> *with that of the other. When a man and*
> *woman unite for the same purpose, which is*
> *enjoyment, it would appear mistaken to say that*
> *the pleasure they both receive from the union*
> *could be of a different nature.*

VATSYAYANA

Everyone did it, but hardly anyone talked about it. There are many glancing references to cunnilingus and fellatio in the *Kama Sutra*, and one short chapter is devoted to perfecting one's fellatio technique. This chapter also reminds the reader that local customs vary—what's widely accepted in one area may be frowned upon in another. Our metrosexual Brahman is advised to take his cues by observing others. That's still good advice.

Oral sex—giving it, getting it—is not to everyone's liking. And it does take some practice to learn how to do it well. However, when practiced with sensitivity and finesse, it's one of the most explosively pleasurable sexual experiences.

FELLATIO

Apparently, the most skilled practitioners of fellatio in ancient India were male prostitutes, who did a brisk trade. The *Kama Sutra* describes a typical encounter with one of these prostitutes. Although in the twenty-first century you are likely having sex with a willing (as opposed to paid) partner of the opposite sex, the techniques are the same.

Whether you are the giver or the receiver, it's important to take things slowly. The tempo is controlled by the giver. Oral sex can be the natural outgrowth of a massage, or of a series of kisses down your lover's body. Move inexorably closer to your target, but teasingly avoid direct contact with the penis. If he doesn't already have an erection, he probably will very soon!

Because fellatio is so pleasurable for the man, frequent stops and starts are a must, or it's possible that you could bring him to orgasm in record time. You can do this deliberately if you want to—for example, if you're going for a lunchtime quickie—but be aware of the awesome power of your mouth and tongue when they come into contact with your lover's penis.

FELLATIO TECHNIQUES

The ancients utilized eight techniques of fellatio, progressing as always, in ascending order of intensity.

The Nominal Congress

Touch your lips to your lover's penis while stroking and squeezing it with your hand. You can start with a simple, chaste kiss, or pucker your lips to bring more of your mouth into contact with the penis. This stage is intended to be a "preview of coming attractions."

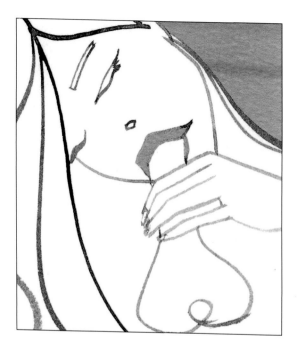

Nibbling the Sides

Place your hand over the head of the penis—perhaps using a gentle massaging motion—while pressing your lips to the sides. Beyond the barest little nibble, use of the teeth is not recommended.

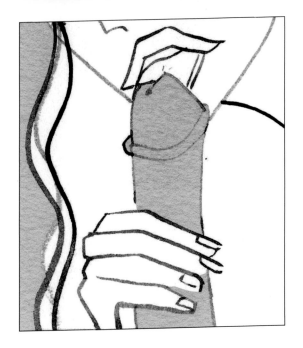

Outside Pressing

Take the end of your lover's penis between your lips, sucking lightly while pressing the sides with your hand.

Inside Pressing

Take a little more of the penis into your mouth and press rhythmically with your lips while moving it in and out.

The Kissing Hold

This differs from **The Nominal Congress** (see page 66) in that you encircle your lover's penis with your hand and hold it still while you kiss it. Again, round your lips to bring the inside of your mouth into contact with the penis, or move your lips along its length, maintaining constant contact.

Polishing

Use your tongue to tease the end of your lover's penis, especially around the end and the sensitive glans. Little butterfly-like flicks are effective, as are licks and swirling motions. Try varying the tongue pressure, either at random, or rhythmically.

Sucking the Mango Fruit

Take about half the length of the penis into your mouth. Now, suck and press with your tongue, as if you were enjoying an especially juicy fruit. You can also swirl your tongue over the end, on the sides, or near the base.

Devouring

Take as much of your lover's penis as you can into your mouth. Again, as the giver of this pleasure, feel free to set your own limits here. Press with your lips, use your tongue, and suck wherever you like. The *Kama Sutra* indicates that tongue pressure alone is usually sufficient to bring a man to orgasm using this technique.

FELLATIO POSITIONS

The *Kama Sutra* neglects to list the positions assumed by the parties when fellatio is being performed, concentrating only on technique. Here are our ideas for what these positions might be named.

The Supplicant

The woman kneels before her partner, who is standing or leaning against a wall. This position enables the man to touch his partner's face, hair, and breasts while she pleasures him.

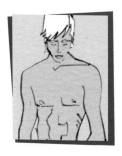

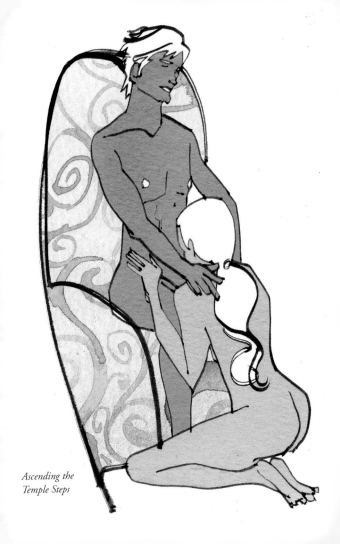

Ascending the Temple Steps

Ascending the Temple Steps

So named because the couple in profile resembles a staircase. Again, the woman kneels, although this time her lover is seated. This may be more comfortable for the man, who doesn't have to worry about keeping his balance at a crucial moment. In any of the kneeling positions, the woman should use a cushion for her knees.

The Silk Road

With the man lying on his back, the woman lies or kneels between her partner's thighs. This position affords a great deal of control to the woman, who is able to move closer or withdraw at will, while the man can relax in a relatively submissive position. From this position, it's also possible to reach your partner's nipples to stroke them—and he can reach yours as well.

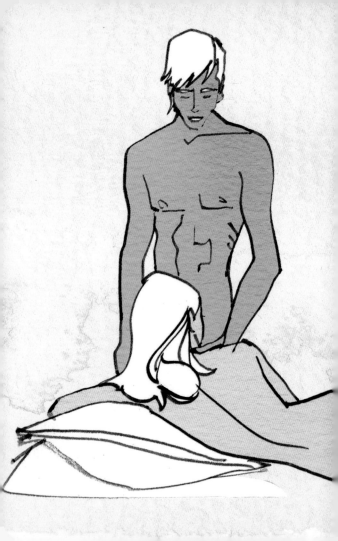

The Insistent Congress

In this position, the woman lies on her side while the man approaches her from a standing or kneeling position. If kneeling, he will have easy access to his lover's face, breasts, and genitals. This is a low-impact position for the woman— no shoulder or knee strain—but to be avoided if he's likely to topple over in the heat of passion.

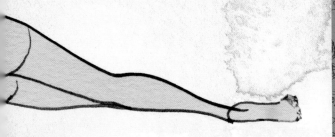

CUNNILINGUS

*Oh, you men who seek for the love and
affection of women and desire to retain them,
see that you frolic before copulation. Prepare
her for the enjoyment and let nothing be
neglected to attain this end. Explore her
with all possible activity, and while so doing,
let your mind be free from all other thought.*

SHEIKH NEFZAWI

As with fellatio, the practice of cunnilingus is
alluded to outside the context of "normal" relationships, although it's acknowledged to have been
widely practiced—and so desired by women that

they would be prepared to
abandon their conventional
relationships in order to obtain
it. In this case, the discussion
centers primarily on the behavior of lesbians. The authors
hedge their bets on the morality
of the act, reverting to the "it's

OK between consenting adults and if it's customary within the culture" evasion. And that's where we are today: There's no reason why willing partners shouldn't enjoy this pleasure. Pace yourselves according to your comfort level.

Some would argue that a woman's genitals resemble an orchid. We won't disagree, but we will suggest that even if you don't believe it looks like an orchid, please treat it as if it were. The little clitoris possesses as many nerve endings as a penis. It often requires a delicate touch or indirect stimulation.

Because no cunnilingus specifics are mentioned in the *Kama Sutra*, we've put a few choice words into Vatsyayana's mouth (so to speak). Consider the following positions and techniques.

CUNNILINGUS POSITIONS

The Mountain Pass

Often, the most comfortable position in which to enjoy cunnilingus is for the woman to lie on her back while her lover lies or kneels between her parted thighs. It also evolves naturally during other forms of foreplay—he moves down her body (or is forcibly pushed), leaving a trail of kisses as he goes. This position will allow the woman to direct her partner's hands and mouth to where (and how) she would like to be touched.

The Moonlit Lotus

So named because the woman's vertical position resembles the tightly closed lotus when it's closed up for the night. The woman either squats or kneels, straddling her lover's head as he lies on his back. This position allows the woman to control the amount of stimulation she receives, moving closer or farther away, as she wishes. If she faces forward, towards her lover's feet, she can bend at the waist—enabling her to touch her partner's nipples, genitals, and to place her breasts in easy reach of his hands.

- The man may use any combination of fingers and tongue to heighten his lady's pleasure.

- This position requires good control of the inner thigh muscles.

The Bridge

In this position, the woman rests on her hands and knees, facing away from her lover, while he kneels behind her. Although some women find this position impersonal because they can't see their partners, it can add an extra dimension of excitement—because she can't be sure what he's going to do next.

- The man has a hand free for additional genital—or even anal—stimulation.

- By leaning forward or back, the woman can vary the type and intensity of stimulation she receives.

CUNNILINGUS TECHNIQUES

Tickling with a Feather

This is a slow, gentle way to get things started. Use your fingertips and the tip of your tongue to tease your way around the labia. As the name suggests, light, feathery strokes are the key. Also, don't neglect the insides of the thighs or the pubic area.

Plucking the Orchid

Again using a delicate touch, use one or more fingers to part the outer labia, exposing the inner labia and clitoris. Continue with small tongue flicks of varying length and pressure, and alternat-

ing with finger strokes. Avoid direct stimulation of the tip of the clitoris unless your partner asks for it. As her level of arousal increases, her lover can move his fingers and tongue a little faster, or press a little harder.

Many women also respond to stimulation of the perineum with finger or tongue.

The Elephant's Trunk

This technique involves deeper insertion of the tongue between the labia and into the vagina. Alternate darting, playful strokes with longer, sustained tongue caresses.

The Willow

It's often possible to bring a woman to orgasm using nothing but indirect stimulation of the clitoris. Using the sides of your tongue and a sawing motion, alternate long, sensuous strokes along the shaft of the clitoris. This stroke can be used in combination with the other techniques listed here to create an endless—and explosively pleasurable—variety of sensations.

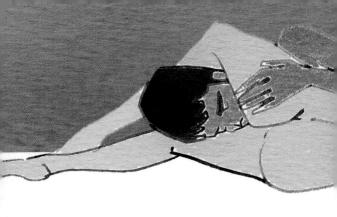

WHEN THE FEELING'S MUTUAL

The Congress of a Crow

Performing simultaneous oral sex on each other satisfies a basic desire to give as good as we get—pleasuring your partner while your partner is pleasuring you. Instead of telling him what you want, *show* him by doing it to him. He's sure to get the idea!

Sometimes this position allows both partners to scale the heights of passion and even culminate in simultaneous orgasm. However, it's equally likely that if you're focused on your partner's

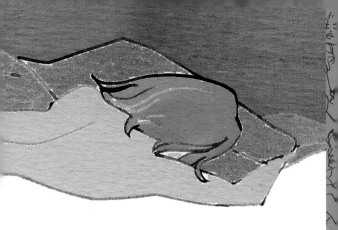

pleasure, you're less apt to be concentrating on your own, and vice versa. If pleasure—giving it or receiving it—becomes a distraction, it's better to use this technique occasionally, or only for short periods. That way you can devote your full attention to the sensations occurring in your own body and be able to reciprocate in full measure with your lover.

Kaka [crow] comes from a root meaning "laulia," an excess of ardor.

YASHODHARA

"Brokeback Mountain" in the Himalayas

Same-gender love in the time of the *Kama Sutra*

> *Citizens with this kind of inclination,*
> *who renounce women and can do without*
> *them willingly because they love each other,*
> *get married together, bound by a deep*
> *and trusting friendship.*

YASHODHARA

As prostitution was common to both sexes, so too was homosexuality. Gender lines were blurred or even erased in a variety of situations. Apparently cross-dressing was popular among young male "shampooers," who were the equivalents of modern-day workers in massage parlors. It was to these shampoo boys that the citizen could go to have his fellatio needs attended to.

"Women acting the part of men"—sexually assertive women—were also known to pursue other women for sexual purposes. The *Kama Sutra* devotes an entire chapter to the sexually assertive woman and the techniques she uses on her partners, both male and female, although the authors appear mildly disapproving of such behavior.

Sometimes circumstances forced women's hands. In royal households, plural marriage was common: the harem. Being sequestered in the harem didn't condemn a woman to celibacy or near-celibacy. The *Kama Sutra* describes a variety of ways the wives could harmlessly amuse themselves and each other using toys and the occasional root vegetable.

It's clear, though, that during the time of the *Kama Sutra*, same-sex love was looked upon as just an aspect of our multifaceted sexuality.

the pleasure principles
intercourse positions and techniques

The characteristics of love are the total
gift of self, the fact of having mutual tastes,
of doing what pleases the other, total
trust, indifference to money.

VATSYAYANA

N ow that you have teased and tantalized each other for hours (or at least for several minutes) with kisses, embraces, and other pleasures, you're probably ready—nay, eager—for intercourse. Not so fast! The *Kama Sutra* is quick to point out that once passion seizes the lovers, they cease to be bound by any rules or conventions. While we still have your attention, we're going to show you the fabled positions of the *Kama Sutra*. Chances are, you've been practicing many of them for years without realizing that you were following in the footsteps of the ancients.

To provide you with the most comprehensive overview and greatest variety of these positions—and their charmingly poetic names—we'll be citing the other ancient texts: *Ananga-Ranga*, *The Perfumed Garden*, and the *T'ung Hsüan Tzu* or *Tao*, as well as the main text of the *Kama Sutra*.

To Make the Missionaries Blush

Man-on-Top Positions

When a man's love is carried to its highest pitch,
all the pleasures of coition become easy for him,
and he satisfies them by embracing and kissing.
There is the real source of happiness for both.

SHEIKH NEFZAWI

The Widely Opened Position

SOURCE: *Kama Sutra*

While lying on her back, the woman bends her knees and arches her back to meet her partner's thrusts. She spreads her legs wide.

- Spreading her legs ensures both deep penetration and clitoral stimulation.

- The woman's hands are free, allowing her to touch her partner's face, hair, or nipples.

- Arching for long periods can be tough on the back. She should brace herself with her feet, and alternate with other positions.

Yawning Position

SOURCE: *Kama Sutra*

The man kneels while the woman lies on her back. She raises her outstretched legs to form a "V."

- Penetration not especially deep.

- Minimal clitoral stimulation. Because the man supports himself on his hands (or is holding hers), manual stimulation is also unlikely.

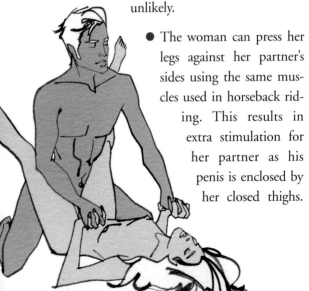

- The woman can press her legs against her partner's sides using the same muscles used in horseback riding. This results in extra stimulation for her partner as his penis is enclosed by her closed thighs.

- High visual appeal: The man has a full view of his supine partner.

Variant Yawning Position

SOURCE: *Kama Sutra*

The woman brings her legs forward, toward her own body. She can bring her knees to her chest, but her legs should remain extended.

- Penetration is much deeper because the angle of the vagina is drawn upward.

- Better clitoral stimulation due to deep penetration.

- Because penetration is deep, the woman should be fully aroused and well-lubricated before attempting this position. If she is on the dry side, she should use a water-soluble lubricant.

The Refined Position

SOURCE: *Ananga-Ranga*

This is one of the *uttana-bandha*, or supine postures. The woman arches her back as in **The Widely Opened Position**, but her partner kneels, and can support her weight on his thighs.

- It's a "hands free-for-all." His hands can roam at will, while the woman has the entire upper half of her lover's body to play with.

- By placing his hands on her hips, he can also move her forward or back.

- If he uses his hands to raise her hips, he increases the odds of hitting the G-spot jackpot (see pages 142-43).

The Gaping Position

SOURCE: *Ananga-Ranga*

In this position, pillows are used to support the woman's lower back and tilt the vagina. If needed, the man can also kneel on pillows to achieve the correct height.

- Because the vagina is exposed, it can receive more stimulation from both the penis and fingers (hers or his).

The Clasping Position

SOURCE: *Kama Sutra*

The man simply lies on top of the woman while she embraces him. Their legs intertwine.

- This is a great position for sustained kissing and nuzzling. With their mouths close to each other's ears, they can whisper romantic endearments or talk dirty.

- Maximum body contact: This is the true meaning of "skin-to-skin."

The Pressing Position

SOURCE: *Kama Sutra*

This is a natural outgrowth of **The Clasping Position**. As the lovers' level of arousal increases, the woman spreads her legs wider and grips her partner with her thighs, while he raises himself on his hands to achieve deeper penetration.

- She can squeeze her thighs rhythmically and twine her legs around her partner's calves to vary his sensations.

- Her hands are also free to stroke his upper body.

- Kissing, nuzzling, and whispering are still possible because their heads are positioned close together.

The Twining Position

SOURCE: *Kama Sutra*

In this variant of **The Pressing Position**, the woman wraps one leg around the man's thigh—pressing him into her.

- This is another deeply intimate position that affords a high level of skin contact.

- Although she lies on her back—usually a more passive position—the woman can exert some control over the speed and depth of her partner's thrusts by using her leg.

The Placid Embrace

SOURCE: *Ananga-Ranga*

Kneeling, the man supports his partner's back and buttocks as he enters her. She wraps her legs around her lover's waist and clasps him around the neck.

- She can pull him deeply inside her with her legs.

- Because he supports her with his hands, it might feel like she's being cradled.

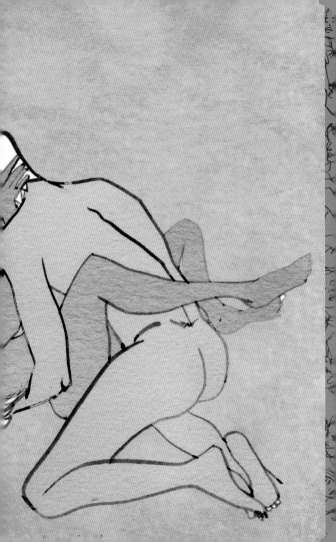

The Rising Position

SOURCE: *Kama Sutra*

The woman raises her legs at a right angle to her body, keeping her knees together. Her lover enters her from a kneeling position. She can rest her ankles on his shoulders.

- This position brings the super-sensitive backs of the knees into play.

- When the woman squeezes her thighs together, she creates friction on her partner's penis—heightening sensations for both partners.

The Queen of Heaven

SOURCE: *Kama Sutra*

Indrani, the Queen of Heaven, was the transcendent wife of the rain and thunder god Indra—one of the Vedic pantheon of early Hindu mythology. Perhaps Indra creates rainy days so he can enjoy these gentle pursuits with his wife without interruption.

- The woman brings her knees to her chest and presses her calves against the backs of her thighs, forming a tightly curled ball. While her partner kneels, he braces himself with his hands on the backs of her thighs. She can rest her feet against his chest as he thrusts.

- The compacted position effectively shortens the vagina and ensures a buildup of sexual tension in the vaginal muscles, which can eventually enhance the woman's orgasms.

- Because this position allows deep penetration, women should be sure that they're fully aroused and lubricated.

- Both partners need to be flexible and limber to achieve this position. If anything feels uncomfortable, stop at once and move on to a less demanding position.

The Raised Feet Posture

SOURCE: *Ananga-Ranga*

The man enters his lover from a kneeling position as she brings her knees close to her chest. Unlike **The Queen of Heaven** (see pages 106-07), she keeps her feet apart, near her partner's waist.

- This position is less strenuous for the woman than **The Queen of Heaven**.

- The man can bend over his lover and fondle her breasts or touch her face because he isn't holding her up.

- If he raises her hips with his hands, his penis will stimulate the front wall of the vagina—the fabled G-spot (see pages 142-43).

SAFETY FIRST (AND LAST)

Sex involves a high level of trust between lovers. Practicing "safe sex" helps prevent pregnancy and sexually-transmitted diseases such as the HIV virus—obviously unheard-of in Vatsyayana's day. It's difficult to trust your partner or ascend the heights of passion if you are worried about either of these conditions.

Although new lovers usually don't know each other's sexual history, both bear responsibility for ensuring a safe sexual experience. Use condoms (male or female) and dental dams (a latex barrier used to protect the mouth and teeth) to protect yourselves from diseases and unplanned pregnancy. Condom use can even become part of your erotic repertoire. Another option is to practice non-penetrative sex, including mutual masturbation—with or without clothing.

Some lovers in committed relationships maintain safe sexual practices indefinitely in order to promote relaxation, trust, and pleasure.

The Level Feet Posture

SOURCE: *Ananga-Ranga*

This is similar to **The Raised Feet Posture** (see pages 108-09), except that the woman extends her legs and rests them on her lover's shoulders. She can bring her knees closer together or farther apart to vary the depth of penetration and the amount of friction on her lover's penis. The man lifts the woman's lower torso until her buttocks rest on his thighs. He is then completely in control of the rhythm of his thrusts.

- Because of the level of control enjoyed by the man, the woman takes a less active role. She won't be able to move very much.

- Although his hands will be occupied holding her waist, she can stroke his arms and chest.

The Pressed Position

SOURCE: *Kama Sutra*

This is exactly what it sounds like. In this position, similar to **The Queen of Heaven** (see pages 106-107), the placement of the woman's feet is important. The soles should rest on her lover's upper chest. Instead of clasping his partner's knees to maintain the compacted posture, the man's hands can roam.

- Although lying on her back can make the woman feel vulnerable or even submissive, the woman can control her partner's thrusts by pressing against him with her feet.

- As with any of the deep-penetration positions, the man needs to be sensitive to his lover's arousal level to avoid discomfort.

- Fingers are not the only digits that can stroke. There's no reason not to tease her lover's nipples with her toes.

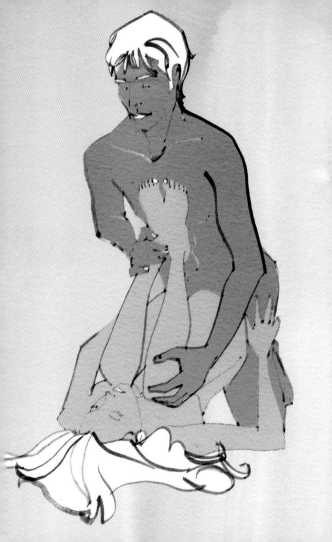

The Half-Pressed Position

SOURCE: *Kama Sutra*

From **The Pressed Position** (see pages 112-13), the woman stretches out one leg behind her partner.

- This position allows more freedom of movement for the woman, who can rotate her hips or generate movement with her stretched-out leg.

- Stretching her leg out can relieve fatigue and expose the clitoris to stimulation.

- This position can be used to change the tempo to a more languid pace.

The Crab's Position

SOURCE: *Kama Sutra*

As its name suggests, this position involves the woman folding her legs back like a crab's claws. As her partner kneels before her, he can hold onto her knees to balance himself.

- This position is less demanding than some of the other "folded up" positions because the man supports his lover's legs.

- As in other raised knee positions, the vagina is constricted, resulting in intense pleasure for both partners.

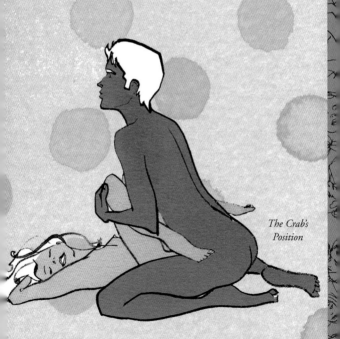

The Crab's Position

The Splitting of a Bamboo

SOURCE: *Kama Sutra*

Not so much a position as a sequence of movements, this position calls for the woman to stretch out one leg and rest it on her partner's shoulder, with the other extended on the bed. She then switches legs, raising first one, then the other, increasing or decreasing the tempo in order to accelerate or delay her lover's climax.

- If she can't fully extend her leg on the man's shoulder, she can bend her knee.

- The man can kneel, kneel with one leg extended, or extend both legs, resting on his hands. The lower his torso is, the easier it will be for his lover to rest her leg on his shoulder.

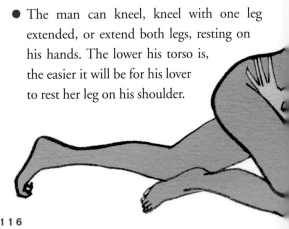

The Fixing of a Nail

SOURCE: *Kama Sutra*

In a slight variation of **The Splitting of a Bamboo**, the woman "fixes" her heel on her lover's forehead. Only attempt this position when you're fresh out of the shower.

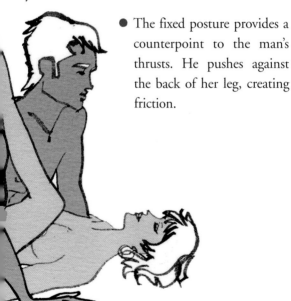

- The fixed posture provides a counterpoint to the man's thrusts. He pushes against the back of her leg, creating friction.

The Splitting of a Bamboo

The Seventh Posture

SOURCE: *The Perfumed Garden*

The man sits on his heels, straddling his lover while she raises one leg crosswise across his chest, resting her ankle on the opposite shoulder. Alternatively, the woman can lie on her side, but this is more difficult.

- If the woman is supple, she can alternate between lying on her back and her side.

- From this position, the man can caress his partner's calf, the backs of her knees, or fondle her breasts.

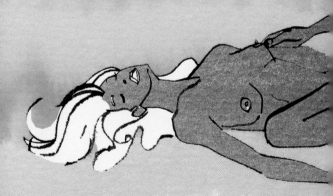

The Encircling Position

SOURCE: *Ananga-Ranga*

The woman lies on her back, "encircling" her vagina with her crossed legs. Her lover must support himself on his hands to avoid exerting too much pressure on her folded legs.

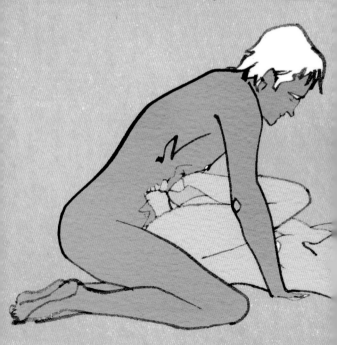

- In this position, there is an element of vulnerability that appeals to many women. Men will also get a charge from the visual stimulus provided by the "framed" vagina.

- Although penetration isn't deep, her clitoris is exposed to stimulation from the movement of intercourse.

FOR EXTRA CREDIT:

The Lotus-Like Position

SOURCE: *Kama Sutra*

Ladies: Lie on your back and assume the lotus position, exposing your vagina. Your yoga instructor will be so proud. No bonus points to your lover, who enters you from a kneeling position and isn't required to do anything special.

The Encircling Position

MEASURE FOR MEASURE

Woman-on-Top and Sitting Positions

Both man and woman should contend against any reserve, or false shame, giving themselves up in complete nakedness to unrestrained voluptuousness, upon a high and handsome bedstead, raised on tall legs, furnished with many pillows, and covered by a rich chatra, or canopy; the sheets being besprinkled with flowers and the coverlet scented by burning luscious incense, such as aloes and other fragrant woods. In such a place, let the man, ascending the throne of love, enjoy the woman in ease and comfort, gratifying his and her every wish and every whim.

SHEIKH NEFZAWI

They called it "the woman acting the part of the man": suitably employed after the man has already experienced one orgasm, but the woman has not yet climaxed, or desires greater erotic fulfillment. The ancients knew, as we know now, that women are slower to ignite and burn longer than men.

Power games were also popular in ancient bedrooms. Women "vanquished" their lovers by forcing them into a supine position and having their way with them. There is sound physiology in this. When the woman is on top, she can position herself to expose her clitoris to stimulation by her man's erect penis. She can also keep her own rhythm and bring herself to orgasm with very little assistance from him.

These positions are better represented—and without the gender bias—in the later texts of *Ananga-Ranga* and *The Perfumed Garden* than they are in the original *Kama Sutra*.

Whether it's her turn to be in charge, and she has him at her mercy, or he's content to lie back and let his lady do all the work, these positions offer rewarding pleasures.

Kama's Wheel

SOURCE: *Ananga-Ranga*

Reportedly "very much enjoyed by the voluptuary," in this position the couple is seated with the woman astride her partner. Their legs, extended straight out, form the shape of an "X"—the spokes of "Kama's Wheel."

- The couple can fondle, kiss, and embrace each other in this intimate face-to-face position.

- The man maintains some control because he can move his lover's hips as he holds her, although the woman is free to move up and down or rotate her hips to suit her own needs.

The Lotus Position

SOURCE: *Ananga-Ranga*

In another of *Ananga-Ranga's upavishta*, or sitting positions, the woman's legs are again extended, although this time the man sits cross-legged in the lotus position (if he can manage it).

- This is another position that affords maximum upper body contact—along with maximum face-to-face intimacy.

- In between wrapping their arms around each other, their hands will be free to fondle their lover's face, nipples, and genitals.

- The clitoris can easily be reached by both lovers.

KEGEL EXERCISES
Why "PC" Is Good for You

These simple exercises strengthen the PC (pubo-coccygeal) muscle and can greatly increase a woman's enjoyment during sex by enabling her to practice the tightening techniques described in the *Kama Sutra*. Women can learn the location and "feel" of this muscle as they urinate. Practice stopping the flow midstream to learn the basic techniques of tightening the muscle. It is easy to practice these exercises any time, repeating a series of tighten-and-release contractions several times a day. You can also gauge the strength of the muscle contractions using your finger. Kegel exercises are especially useful after childbirth, to tone and recondition stretched muscles.

Of course you needn't limit yourself to using these techniques only in the positions where they're mentioned. In this case, more is *definitely* better—just ask your man, preferably when he's in a position not to argue.

The Accomplishing Position

SOURCE: *Ananga-Ranga*

Instead of extending her legs behind her lover as in **Kama's Wheel** and **The Lotus Position** (see pages 124-26), the woman raises one leg and bends the other while her lover sits in the cross-legged posture.

- Their upper bodies will be pressed together quite tightly in this position. Pelvic movement, especially the man's, will be restricted. However, this position is useful for continuing intercourse when either or both of them have already had an orgasm but wish to resume slowly. It's also good for taking a breather after one of the more strenuous positions.

- By changing the height of her raised leg, or by raising her legs alternately, the woman can create friction on her lover's penis.

The Swing

SOURCE: *Kama Sutra*

Facing her lover's feet, the woman straddles her lover, who either lies flat or braces himself on his arms.

- The woman can lean forward, back, or sit straight up to vary the depth of penetration. Moving her pelvis exposes her clitoris to friction from her lover's penis.

- While some might consider this position somewhat impersonal because the couple doesn't face one another, the man enjoys a visually appealing view of his lover's back and buttocks.

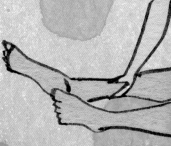

The Pair of Tongs

SOURCE: *Kama Sutra*

This combination of position and technique can
be exquisitely satisfying for both partners. The
woman kneels astride her partner, facing
him, while he lies on his back.
Raising his knees is optional,
although that can provide a
place for her to lean back.
Using her PC (pubo-
coccygeal) muscle, the
woman contracts her
vagina rhythmically

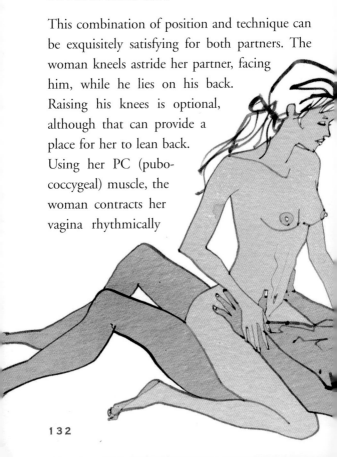

around her lover's penis, creating a powerfully erotic sensation for both.

- This position is all about the woman—she's in charge of how to move, how fast, and how deep she wants penetration to be.

- The man's hands are free to stroke and fondle his partner virtually anywhere on her body. Depending on the angle at which she sets herself, the woman may also have a free hand to manually stimulate her own clitoris, or touch her lover's body.

- By sitting straight up and contracting her PC muscle, the woman draws her lover's penis very deeply inside.

The Position of Equals

SOURCE: *Ananga-Ranga*

As the woman sits astride her lover, she wraps her legs around his back, hooking her ankles together. She can lean back and support herself on her arms, allowing her partner easy access to her breasts.

- She can also use her thigh muscles to hold her lover's waist. The tighter she holds him, the deeper penetration will be.

- Because she sits on his thighs, the man's pelvic movements are restricted. The woman controls the speed of intercourse and the depth of penetration.

- This position can cause lower back fatigue, especially for the man. Try alternating with one of the lying-down positions.

The Snake Trap

SOURCE: *Ananga-Ranga*

Seated facing each other, woman astride, the lovers lean back and grasp each other's ankles.

- Great visuals for both partners. This is one of the few positions where you can comfortably watch yourself making love—or you can simply gaze into your lover's eyes.

- The rocking motion engendered by this position doesn't allow for deep penetration, but is better suited as an interim cooling down in between more demanding positions.

- Instead of being tightly compressed, as in other positions, your bodies are stretched, creating a different series of sensations.

The Orgasmic Role Reversal

SOURCE: *Ananga-Ranga*

As its name suggests, this is a position where the woman can achieve an orgasm with very little effort on the part of her man, who may already be spent from an orgasm of his own. She squats over her lover's penis and moves both up and down and from side to side.

- The squatting position contracts the vagina, increasing the buildup of sexual tension.

- Keeping her thighs tightly closed also increases friction.

- Speed, angle, and depth of penetration are all up to the woman.

The Ascending Position

SOURCE: *Ananga-Ranga*

In this position, the woman is definitely in the "ascendancy." She sits cross-legged on her partner's thighs and lowers herself onto his penis.

- As in most of the other woman-on-top positions, the man's hands are free to stroke and fondle his lover.

- This position requires a little balance, so the woman may need to support herself with one or both arms on her partner's legs.

- The forward-tilted angle of her vagina may help to stimulate her G-spot.

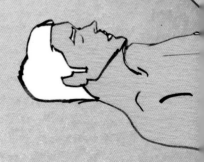

HITTING THE RIGHT NOTE
The Elusive "G"

What's the G-spot? It's a myth, right? Wrong. While it is true that not every woman has a G-spot, and not everyone who has one responds to having it stimulated, many women experience powerful orgasms via their G-spot.

The G-spot, also known by its official name, the Grafenberg spot, is an exquisitely sensitive area on the front wall of the vagina, a little more than halfway between the entrance of the vagina and the cervix. Although all the facts are not yet in, it is thought to have a function similar to a man's prostate gland.

How to find yours, or know whether you have one? Let your fingers do the walking. With your palm facing toward your pubic bone, insert one or two fingers in your vagina. Using your fingertips, locate a raised spot or ridge along the front wall of your vagina—although the spot may

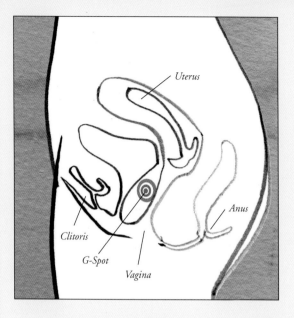

be difficult to feel at first. You may feel incredible pleasure, but don't be surprised if it's accompanied by a powerful urge to pee!

Finally, don't be discouraged if your G-spot doesn't turn out to be a "magic pleasure button." You already have one: your clitoris. But if you are one of the lucky ones—if you've got it, flaunt it.

Interchange in Coition

SOURCE: *The Perfumed Garden*

Think "push-ups plus." The woman lies facedown on her partner and squeezes her vagina and thighs around his penis. She props herself on her arms, using them to move up and down.

- The woman may need to lie with her thighs on a cushion to help raise her pelvis to a height suitable for intercourse.

- This position provides upper-body contact and opportunity for kissing often missing from woman-on-top positions.

- Women who are a little short on upper-body strength will tire quickly in this position.

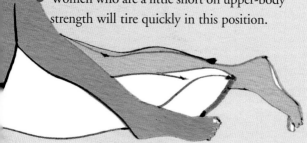

The Fitter-In

SOURCE: *The Perfumed Garden*

Similar to **The Snake Trap** (see pages 136-37), this position has the lovers intertwining their legs in an "over-under" manner: her right leg over his left thigh; his right leg over her left thigh, which creates both a pleasing symmetry and a languid rocking rhythm.

- Hold each other by the arms.

- To derive optimum pleasure from this position, the lovers should be completely in sync with each other emotionally and physically.

The Goat and the Tree

SOURCE: *T'ung Hsüan Tzu*

In this sitting position, the woman straddles the man's lap while he is seated on a chair.

- To sustain this position, the man should sit on a chair with back support.

- His hands are free to fondle his lover's breasts and clitoris—and she can do the same for herself.

- The woman should brace her feet on the floor in order to move up and down on her partner's penis.

- The lovers can either be face-to-face, or the woman can face away from her man.

EASY LIKE SUNDAY MORNING

Side-by-Side Positions

It is advisable that the connoisseur of copulation should try all the postures so that he may know which gives pleasure to the woman.

SHEIKH NEFZAWI

There's a relaxed equality to these face-to-face positions that often arises naturally when the lovers are sleepy. Don't be fooled, though; the side-by-side positions definitely deliver the goods. They can be every bit as pleasurable as their more athletic cousins.

The Side-by-Side Clasping Position

SOURCE: *Kama Sutra*

Like the related **Clasping Position** (see pages 98-99), there's an element of twining your limbs around your lover that's both lyrical and romantic. (Did we also mention sexy?)

- This position allows for virtually head-to-foot body contact.

- Let your hands roam freely . . . wherever they want. Touch your partner where you would like to be touched.

- Shallow penetration can be either a prelude to more intense lovemaking, or a gentle slowdown.

The Crab Embrace

SOURCE: *Ananga-Ranga*

In this position, the man lies between his lover's thighs while she helps him to enter her by throwing her leg across his body, resting on his hip or waist.

- The higher she raises her leg, the more deeply she allows her lover to penetrate.

- If the man braces his knees on the bed, he can also have some thrusting traction.

- It's amazing the amount of fun to be had with one free hand apiece.

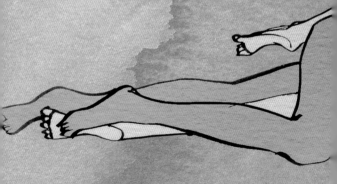

Drawing the Bow

SOURCE: *The Perfumed Garden*

The lovers form an "X" with the woman facing toward her partner's feet and her legs extended behind his back. She raises one leg and he enters her, bending slightly at the waist.

- To make this position work, you need to hang onto each other; the man must hold his lover's shoulders.

- Although it's unlikely to become your favorite position, this position has novelty value and is good for a change of pace.

ANIMAL INSTINCTS
Standing and Rear-Entry Positions

Sexual relations can be diversified
by studying the movements of domestic
and wild animals, as well as insects.

VATSYAYANA

The ancients looked to the animal world for inspiration . . . and found plenty. The *Kama Sutra* encourages lovers to imitate mating animals as a form of play—right down to the sound effects. While we don't advocate bellowing like a bull or snarling like a tiger (at least not if you live in an apartment or are within earshot of small children), low growls, purrs, and chirps of pleasure are sounds that can enhance the erotic experience. So too, the standing and rear-entry positions can become an exciting part of your expanding lovemaking repertoire.

The Suspended Congress

SOURCE: *Kama Sutra*

Prepare to "suspend" your disbelief—this position really can work! The man should use his quadriceps muscles to absorb some of his partner's weight as he leans against a stable support. Ladies, hang on tight… but not so tight that you cause your lover discomfort.

- The woman can also wrap her legs around her partner's waist. This will allow deeper penetration.

- If you are trying this position in the shower, be sure to stand on a nonslip surface.

The Elephant Posture

SOURCE: *Kama Sutra*

In this position, the woman lies facedown while her partner lies over her, supporting himself on his arms. He arches his back as he enters her.

- The woman can create additional friction by moving her thighs closer together or farther apart.

- The man can kiss and nuzzle his lover's back and neck—or turn her on with erotic whisperings into her ear.

The Elephant Posture

The Supported Congress

SOURCE: *Kama Sutra*

Remember the **Climbing a Tree** embrace (see page 40)? Now you know where it can lead. The woman embraces her lover and raises one leg, allowing her lover to enter her from a standing position. She wraps her raised leg around him. For this position to be more than just a tease, lean against a wall.

- If the man is much taller than the woman, this will be a difficult position to maintain, especially as the woman needs to keep her legs spread, further reducing her height.

- The standing positions allow for a great deal of body and face-to-face contact, although your hands will probably be occupied just holding yourselves up.

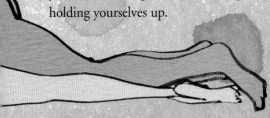

The Congress of a Cow

SOURCE: *Kama Sutra*

The woman bends at the waist, keeping her legs straight, and braces her hands on the floor while her lover thrusts from behind.

- The man sets the pace, holding his partner by the waist and moving her back and forth.

- He can also reach around to stimulate her breasts and clitoris with one or both hands—although the position becomes difficult to control if he's not holding her waist.

- If the woman has trouble touching her toes, she can hold onto a chair or bed instead of reaching all the way down to the floor.

- Keeping her head down will increase the flow of blood to her head—and possibly result in a spectacular orgasm. But the woman should be careful when she stands up, because the sudden change of position could cause dizziness.

The Sixth Posture

SOURCE: *The Perfumed Garden*

This position is straightforward, with both partners kneeling. The woman can keep her back straight or angle forward with her head resting on the bed . . . or anywhere in between.

- If the man isn't using his hands to hold his lover's waist, he can fondle her breasts or even reach around to her clitoris.

- Protect your knees with a cushion if you're doing this on the floor.

- Although the rear-entry positions could be considered impersonal because they don't offer face-to-face contact, they make up for it with a level of raw eroticism of the "do it to me now!" variety.

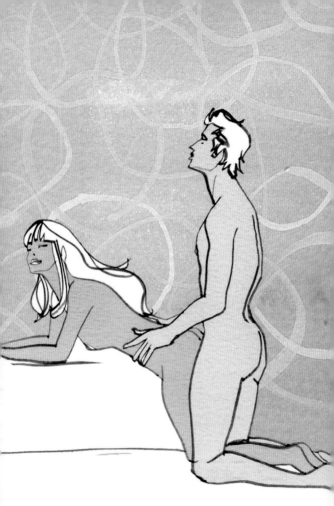

The Ninth Posture

SOURCE: *The Perfumed Garden*

In this position, the man enters his partner as she kneels and leans across a surface like a bed . . . or the kitchen table, or her office desk, or the supermarket checkout. . . .

- Variants of this position include a front-entry option wherein the woman lies on the bed (or table, or the hood of the car) on her back, with her feet on the floor.

- The support afforded by the surface provides a counterpoint for the man's thrusts and reduces the need for him to hang onto his partner's waist.

Mandarin Ducks

SOURCE: *T'ung Hsüan Tzu*

Li T'ung Hsüan, author of *T'ung Hsüan Tzu*, named the category of rear-entry positions "The Fish Sunning Itself." Nowadays, we might call this position "spooning" because the lovers nestle together like two spoons in a drawer.

- This position is lower-impact and more relaxed than the other rear-entry positions.

- Also unlike the other rear-entry positions, being able to lie side-by-side on the bed frees the hands for caressing each other.

- Lovers sometimes find themselves spontaneously making love in this position during an early-morning or late-night cuddle.

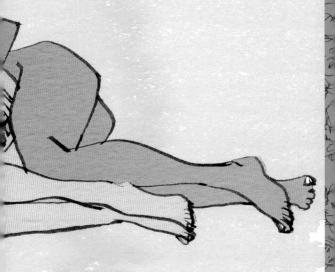

MOTION IN THE OCEAN

The Love Techniques of the *Kama Sutra*

When the mutual operation is performed,
a lively combat ensues between the two actors
who frolic and kiss and intertwine. Enjoyment
is not long delayed, in consequence of the con-
tact of the two pubes. Man, in the pride of his
strength, works like a pestle, and woman, with
lascivious undulations, comes artfully to his aid.
Soon, all too soon, the ejaculation comes!

SHEIKH NEFZAWI

Think of the positions of the *Kama Sutra* as the cinematography of a classic film: visually absorbing, technically flawless, beautiful to watch. Now add the sound track: the movements and techniques that create the explosive magic to transform your sexual experience into a blockbuster.

I HAVE A MAN WHO NEVER NEEDS BATTERIES

General Techniques for Men

All the techniques described here are listed in the *Kama Sutra* in the section entitled "The acts to be done by the man." In the days before battery-operated toys, the author makes clear that the man bears responsibility for satisfying his partner.

- **Moving Forward** is straightforward, in-out intercourse. The vanilla ice cream of sex. Vanilla is important because it's the basis for so many other flavors. Remember that!

- **Churning**: The man holds his penis and moves it in a circular fashion while he's inside his partner.

- **Piercing** means the man enters his partner from above and rubs his penis against her clitoris.

- **Pressing** doesn't involve actual penetration,

but simply pressing the penis against the entrance to the vagina.

- **Giving a Blow:** The man pauses during intercourse, withdraws his penis, and strikes his partner's vagina (gently!).

- **Blow of the Boar** and **Blow of the Bull** are similar. They involve rubbing the penis against one or both sides of the vagina during intercourse.

- **Sporting of a Sparrow** occurs when the man moves his penis rapidly in and out of his lover's vagina, but never fully withdraws.

. . . And a few more, courtesy of *The Perfumed Garden*

- **Love's Tailor:** The man doesn't insert his penis fully, but moves it halfway in and out rapidly (but doesn't withdraw). Then he plunges his penis in as deeply as it will go. For this technique the woman should be fully aroused and lubricated.

- **The Toothpick in the Vulva** is something of a misnomer. (What guy would want to think of himself as a "toothpick?") This technique is similar to the **Churning** described in the *Kama Sutra*, but more vigorous. The man moves his penis in and out, and from side to side.

- **The Encirclement of Love** involves some serious grinding! At full penetration, the man rotates his pelvis (and by extension, his penis) against his lover. With this technique, it's important not to withdraw, but to maintain the deepest penetration.

SISTERS ARE DOING IT
General Techniques for Women

These love techniques were intended to give pleasure to both the woman and her partner, especially when, as often appeared to be the case, the man ran out of steam before his lady. (Maybe that had to do with having so many wives and having to satisfy all of them.)

The Mare's Position

It's not really correct to call it a "position," because this technique can be used in almost any position. Using her PC muscle (see page 127), the woman tenses her vaginal muscles around her lover's penis during intercourse. It can be done as a sustained squeeze, or rhythmically, in waves.

- Experiment with a rhythm that feels good to both you and your lover. Many men report that use of this technique by their partners is explosively pleasurable.

- Ladies, keeping your PC muscle toned can also benefit you. These muscles contract during orgasm. Tighter muscles equal stronger orgasms. Bonus!

The Pair of Tongs

The *Kama Sutra* describes this technique in the context of a straightforward woman-on-top position (see pages 132-33), although it can be practiced in almost any position that allows for deep penetration. What's important here is that the woman tightens her PC muscles around her lover's penis to draw it deeply inside her vagina and hold it there. Using this technique, she can drive her partner wild without moving a muscle (except one, that is).

In Sync with Your Instincts

Love Techniques for the Couple

As you practice the positions of the *Kama Sutra* and become comfortable with them, you can try out some of the synchronized techniques described by the ancient love masters. Often these will have the effect of drawing out your pleasure and delaying climax—because if you're focused on following a rhythm, the theory goes, you won't be overtaken by the crescendo of your own orgasm. The buildup of passion deepens the intimacy of your experience and will probably yield spectacular results. The techniques below are all detailed in *The Perfumed Garden*.

The Bucket in the Well

This is almost like a dance step. During intercourse, the man pushes his penis in deeply, then withdraws a little. The woman follows his lead, pushing herself onto his penis and then pulling back. Because this technique requires some concentration, it facilitates the steady buildup of sexual tension.

The Mutual Shock

Shocking? Perhaps it was considered shocking to tease each other this way in ancient times. Or maybe it would be shocking to be able to carry on this technique for very long without succumbing to blinding passion. After penetration, the lovers pull back so that only the head of the penis is still inside the vagina. Then they move together again, driving the penis deep inside. Repeat—for as long as you're able.

The Approach

Here's an erotic version of what we learned in kindergarten: everybody take turns. First, the man moves his penis inside the vagina—either in a circular fashion, or in and out. Then he stops. Then the woman takes a turn, moving around her lover's penis. The trick is to keep still while your partner does the moves.

Kinky
it's in the eye of the beholder

*About these things there cannot be either
enumeration or any definite rule. Congress having
once commenced, passion alone gives birth to all
the acts of the parties. Such passionate actions . . .
during sexual intercourse, cannot be defined,
and are as irregular as dreams.*

KAMA SUTRA

One thing that we can all agree on is that there's no set definition of what it means to be "kinky." It was evident that during the time that the *Kama Sutra* and *Ananga-Ranga* topped the best-seller list, ritualized scratching, slapping, and biting were commonly practiced. We no longer use a laundry list of specialized marks to make on our beloved's skin, each with its own meaning, but most of us have probably sported a "love bite" or hickey at one time or another. Pleasure can be awfully close to pain, and this wasn't news in the fourth century, either.

The *Kama Sutra* explains that bites and nail marks indicate that someone was the "property" of a lover. Both men and women wore their badges proudly, showing them off to their friends. A scratch or bruise also had the power to arouse and evoke the memory of a passionate encounter. Often the text refers to the ritualized combat that preceded

or accompanied intercourse. Kinky? They didn't think so. (Ever make passionate love after a quarrel with your beloved?)

Nowadays, we have abandoned the symbolic meaning of "marking" our lovers (and few people would want to be considered the "property" of their partners), but we can still engage in some rough-and-tumble play to spice up our routines.

Then, as now, the authors make it clear that both parties must practice restraint and respect for the other's boundaries. It's easy to get carried away in the heat of the moment, but if your partner says "quit it," stop at once.

READY TO TAKE A LITTLE WALK ON THE WILD SIDE?

Fingernails were a favorite tool of ancient lovers, who decorated each other with symbolic marks: crescents, circles, and scratches. These could be applied anywhere on the body. Fingernail scratching also featured in the mock aggression that lovers displayed to one another.

- It's not uncommon to use your nails on your partner's back in the throes of passion—it sends the message that "you're doing such a great job that I can't control myself!" Just be careful not to dig into the skin too hard. Ladies should be especially careful if they sport long talons.

- Light fingernail pressure almost anywhere on the body can cause the most delightful shivers, called "horripilation" in the translated text. (Really! We didn't make this word up.)

- Trace a sexy message on your partner's back and see if he can guess what you're trying to spell out. A wrong guess should bear some type of penalty (see spanking, pages 181-82).

Teeth have nibbled out their own small niche in the lovers' repertoire. Biting should always be gentle—more lip and gum than teeth—and care should be taken never to break the skin, because you could risk a nasty infection.

- To give a good love bite, apply sucking pressure to soft skin. The teeth should barely be involved. The longer you suck and the softer the skin (love bites bloom profusely on the tender skin of the neck and throat), the more pronounced the mark.

- You might have guessed that the *Kama Sutra* has names for several different kinds of bites, and specifications about where on the body they are to be applied.

- Playful nips are referred to as **points**. These can be applied singly or in a line along the selected body part.

- Soft, sucking bites with the teeth and lips are called **jewels**, or **coral and jewels**.

- More intense bites that can cause significant skin marks (and that you probably will not want to try) are called the **broken cloud** and the **biting of the boar**.

Advice from the *Kama Sutra* that your mother probably wouldn't approve of: If your lover bites you, bite him back twice as hard! This is bound to cause a lovers' quarrel, after which you can lustily make up. *"Thus if men and women act according to each other's liking, their love for each other will not be lessened even in one hundred years."*

Hands: Care for a little spanky with your hanky-panky? You're not alone. Ritual striking was commonly employed to arouse a partner during Vatsyayana's time. Sex was even compared to a form of combat. War between the sexes notwithstanding, it's not acceptable to strike your lover with a closed hand, in anger, or if he or she objects to this type of love play.

- A light spanking on the buttocks can leave you feeling warm and tingly.

- Tapping or patting the pubic area with your fingers during sex can also increase arousal—the more blood that moves to that part of the body, the greater the erotic sensation.

- The *Kama Sutra* specified a series of sounds intended to accompany these gentle (we hope) blows, including cooing, hissing, and weeping. Apparently "moaning" didn't make it into the *Kama Sutra* Top 10.

- Don't underestimate the power of a good squeeze: to the breasts, nipples, buttocks (one cheek at a time), or even arms and thighs. Try a knee squeeze under the table when you're out somewhere with your partner.

Cross-dressing was practiced by both genders during the time of the *Kama Sutra*, and nobody seemed too concerned about it. Sometimes the cross-dressing took the form of subterfuge, as a man would dress as a female in order to sneak into a lady's quarters. Conceivably, a girl could dress as a boy in order to eavesdrop on some juicy gossip among the guys. Sometimes men dressed as women because they enjoyed it, although there is no mention of women who habitually cross-dressed. Gender role reversal was considered an important part of a healthy sexuality. Trading roles—or clothes—can be both fun and liberating for couples. See how the other half lives—and loves.

Toys: We can only guess what fun the ancients might have had if they'd had access to battery-powered toys. As it was, it appears that every good home sported a dildo, to be employed at the whim of the woman. She could use it to satisfy herself, or to tease her already-sated partner. As lesbian behavior was also common, especially in plural marriage situations, women also used dildos to satisfy each other.

- Toys are fun. (That's why they're called toys.) Follow the *Kama Sutra*'s example and use them as accessories (not surrogates) in your sex life.

- A dildo is basically a fake penis. A vibrator is a fake penis that uses batteries to vibrate, rotate, or otherwise move around.

- Vibrators and dildos can be used inside the vagina—when your lover's penis is occupied elsewhere, for example, or anywhere else on the body where it feels good. Battery-powered vibrators are useful accessories to help bring a woman to orgasm, although there's no reason why men can't use them on their penises (or anywhere else, for that matter).

- Did we mention that toys are fun for girls and boys?

Group sex brings the issue of trust between (or among) lovers to the fore. Unless you're in a plural marriage and really, really dig your co-spouses, group sex, threesomes, and other variations tend to be exceptions—one-time or occasional episodes in a relationship or during your more pedestrian sex life. And with good reason. If you're in a relationship, introducing other people into your sex life can add a dimension of complication, jealousy, and emotion that can be difficult to cope with. In the *Kama Sutra*, group sex is described in playful terms, as if it were an occasional, but not abnormal diversion.

- All variations of group sex appear to have been practiced regularly during the time of the *Kama Sutra*.

- Sometimes group sex consisted of little more than an erotic frolic among a group of friends, although the *Kama Sutra* allows for the possibility that a threesome could be a permanent and viable arrangement.

beyond the boudoir
keeping it real after the big deal

At the end of the congress . . . the lovers
may also sit on the terrace of the palace or
house, and enjoy the moonlight, and carry
on an agreeable conversation. . . .
This is the end of sexual union.

<small>Kama Sutra</small>

The *Kama Sutra* is a really long book. Unabridged editions run more than 500 pages. Of these 500 pages, exactly *one chapter*, or about 14 pages, is devoted to sex positions. Yes, that's all. So what's up with the remaining 486 pages? Easy—it's about relationships. It's about courtship, that old-fashioned word. It's about putting a shy person at ease. It's about making your marriage—whatever kind of marriage it is—work. It's about being the best "you" you can be and, by doing so, honoring and respecting yourself and your partner.

The *Kama Sutra* also offers recipes for love charms (including several to cure impotence), marital advice, and lessons on how to end a relationship. Although these sections are beyond the scope of this book, they're not beyond the scope of the contemporary person's life.

We can take a lesson from the love doctors of 1,600 years ago. The positions are fun. Done right, the positions can lead you to supersonic,

knock-the-walls-down bliss. But the positions are worthless if approached as gymnastic exercises. Despite being a sexually-liberated society, ancient India also practiced a code of conduct embracing mutual respect and admiration between the sexes, without which sexual liberation could easily devolve into debauchery. Yes, there was playtime, and plenty of it, but after playtime, there was conversation, stargazing, and affection. These endure long after the sweat dries on our bodies and the pangs of pleasure subside.

May this treatise . . . be beloved of
Man and Woman . . . as long as Lakshmi
loveth Vishnu; . . . and as long as the Earth,
the Moon and the Sun endure.

KALYANA MALLA, *Ananga-Ranga*

INDEX

PETER PAUPER PRESS
Fine Books and Gifts Since 1928

Our Company

In 1928, at the age of twenty-two, Peter Beilenson began printing books on a small press in the basement of his parents' home in Larchmont, New York. Peter—and later his wife, Edna—sought to create fine books that sold at "prices even a pauper could afford."

Today, still family owned and operated, Peter Pauper Press continues to honor our founders' legacy—and our customers' expectations—of beauty, quality, and value.

Available in this series:

THE LITTLE BLACK BOOKS

OTHER LITTLE BOOKS